Unlock Your Greatness Leadership Coaches Manual

Heather Thane

Lesson Plans That Unlock Greatness

Published by Greatness Publishing, Ontario, Canada
Cover design by Farouk Roberts

Library and Archives Canada
ISBN 978-0-9868878-7-1

www.greatnesspublishing.com

MISSION STATEMENT

TO INSPIRE TEACHERS TO ANALYZE, UNDERSTAND AND

EXPLAIN

THE PRINCIPLES OF LEADERSHIP

AND

UNLOCK THE GREATNESS

IN EVERYONE

PERSONAL ENDORSEMENTS

"My friend has always been on the cutting edge of business communication. A consummate professional with a flair for explaining difficult concepts, she has mastered the art of grabbing your attention, blowing your mind and taking it to the atmosphere. I am excited about this scholarly adventure and guarantee a mouth-watering experience of academic excellence."

--- Gary Steele, Marketer/Trainer

Toronto, ON

"This book will be a great inspiration and resource for experienced and aspiring leaders. Her years of teaching and coaching have culminated in this easy and 'well-thought out' Teaching Manual. Congratulations, keep on doing what you do best!"

--- Andrea Montague, Accountant, Eco Waste Solutions

Hamilton, ON

"Through the effort of the author, a masterpiece has been created, of which the practical and applicable content will impact greatly on the lives of young people for generations to come. May her success continue to soar."

--- Lisa Spencer-Burgess, Teacher

Toronto District School Board

"The author has skilfully transferred her life as a 'natural' teacher and as a motivator in imparting her vision of confidence into the lives of those who have been in her presence. I personally have profited having her as my personal coach and tutor, 'running on the confidence' that she has imparted on me to reach unattainable goals. Anyone who is willing to practice and apply the lessons and interactive exercises in this manual, will also find that they too can, not only reach for the impossible, but also attain it as well."

--- Ruth Greaves-McKenzie, RPN, London, ON

BRE Graduate (Pastoral Ministry)

"The author's outstanding achievement and her continuous desire to share empowering insights with others are awesome. This book was a labor of love for her and will certainly touch the lives of thousands of people."

--- Brenda Sanku, Teacher

Thames Valley District School Board

FOREWORD

When I first met Heather I knew I had met an outstanding master teacher. Her passion for teaching and youth leadership development was obvious.

So it was a natural evolution in our relationship when I asked her to write the lesson plan manual for my Unlock your Greatness Book.

Heather, this lesson plan book is a gem and the best is yet to come. Thanks.

Andre Thomas

CONTENTS

ACKNOWLEDGMENTS

The author wishes to express her love and gratitude to her beloved family – Gordon, Greg, and Cami for their understanding and endless love throughout the duration of this book.

The author would like to express her heartfelt thanks to her parents for their blessings, and her friends for their wishes for the successful completion of the book.

Time had been more than a highly priced commodity, especially during the last phase of this exercise. Special thanks to Bishop Andre Thomas, who was abundantly helpful and offered invaluable guidance.

Thanks to Mark O'Brien for the thoughtful and creative comments that he provided at critical and opportune times.

The author could not have accomplished this task without Mark Bennett, who has supported her all along, and did a great job of editing.

PREFACE

The Road Map to Greatness

This book provides the reader with the sound tested strategies for teaching the "Unlock your Greatness" Program. The strategies and carefully selected activities suggested in each lesson can be taught to students pursuing Leadership courses. Each chapter contains Focusing Events, Teacher Procedures, Case Studies, "Stop and Reflect" Personal Leadership Activities that constitute rich resources or independent study.

As author, I intend for this book to be used by Coaches, Teachers, and Leaders to successfully deliver the "Unlock your Greatness" Program. It is considered a practical guidepost meant to help provide the teachers with the knowledge and tools to cultivate the personal qualities and characteristics that will help them to lead their students to greatness. As teachers, we are challenged more and more to deliver great things in tough times.

LAYING THE PROPER FOUNDATION

Leading yourself is the first step toward serving others and this can be done by "Sharing with your Heart", Sharing with Peace" and "Sharing with your Mind".

Sharing with your Heart – Be a servant to others. Do you have unique skills and/or experiences that have given you wisdom in a particular area? Share with others with the right spirit and rewards will follow. Be inspired before inspiring others. Keep going, despite setbacks and disappointments.

Sharing with Peace – Sow your seeds of harmony. Be quiet and still at times; if we must efficiently lead others we have to lead ourselves first.

Sharing with your Mind – Are you dependable? Do you keep your promises? One is prone to make mistakes, if we do not spend time thinking, reflecting and evaluating.

The author has had frequent requests from young people and colleagues to help them apply the book's principles to their own lives and workplaces. The author dedicates this Manual to all whose lives she has touched; use your Greatness to touch the lives of others, knowing that you can help others to do the same.

CHAPTER 1

INSTRUCTOR/TEACHER:

COURSE TITLE: LEADERSHIP (UNLOCK YOUR GREATNESS PROGRAM)

SUGGESTED GRADES: Grades 8 - 12

UNIT: DEFINE..... THE LEADER IN YOU

LESSON 1

AIM: To introduce the main Principles of Leadership

LEARNING OBJECTIVES

At the end of the lesson, students will be able to:

1. Define the term "Leadership"
2. Identify key attributes of the effective leader

LESSON CONTENT

- Definition of Leadership
- Qualities/Characteristics of an effective Leader
- Habitual Leaders v Situational Leaders

INSTRUCTIONAL PROCEDURES

Focusing Event

Ask students to:

- Think about one person who they regard as being a good, strong leader
- List four things that they think makes this person a strong leader
- List four undesirable leadership qualities
- Write these on the board after consultation with the group

Teaching Procedures

- Introduced the topic by explaining that strong leadership is essential to shape the world around them and ignite greatness in others

Formative Check

Activity: Word Search on Leadership Terms

Student Participation

- Guided Discussions
- Completion of the Word Search
- "Stop and Reflect" in Textbook

EVALUATION PROCEDURES

"Stop and Reflect" – Pages 13 - 15 in Textbook

MATERIALS AND AIDS

- Whiteboard
- Textbook
- Word Search

CLOSURE

Summarize that "The Leader in You" means that a leader will inspire and motivate so that the group is empowered to achieve.

INSTRUCTOR/TEACHER:

COURSE TITLE: LEADERSHIP (UNLOCK YOUR GREATNESS PROGRAM)

SUGGESTED GRADES: Grades 8 - 12

UNIT: DEFINE..... THE LEADER IN YOU

LESSON 2

AIM: To introduce the main Principles of Leadership

LEARNING OBJECTIVES

At the end of the lesson, students will be able to:

1. Define the term "Ideas"
2. Define the term "Visions"
3. List examples of Ideas and Visions
4. Differentiate between Ideas and Visions
5. Assess the importance of Ideas and Visions

LESSON CONTENT

- Definition of Ideas

- Definition of Vision

- Examples of Ideas and Vision

- Importance of Ideas and Vision

INSTRUCTIONAL PROCEDURES

Focusing Event

- Ask students to consider the following question: What would happen if you go on a journey without a map?
- Write answers provided by the students on the board.

Teaching Procedures

- Develop lesson by asking students to complete the following activity:

Draw/Write for three minutes on construction paper, what comes to mind when they read the statement on the board:

"GREAT LEADERS HAVE IDEAS AND VISION"

- Encourage students to draw/write whatever comes to mind:

a) Define it

b) Question it

c) Give Examples

- Students do not have to pay attention to grammar, spelling, etc.

Formative Check

- Pair and Share – Students will be instructed to share their ideas and/or vision with a classmate.

- Discuss as a whole class

Student Participation

- Guided Discussion
- Activity – Mind Map
- Pair and Share
- "Stop and Reflect" in Textbook
- Display of Ideas and Visions on walls around the classroom

EVALUATION PROCEDURES

"Stop and Reflect" – Pages 21 – 23 in Textbook

MATERIALS AND AIDS

- Ideas Chart
- Visions Chart

- Construction Paper

- Textbook

CLOSURE

Students will display their ideas/visions on walls around the classroom

INSTRUCTOR/TEACHER:

COURSE TITLE: LEADERSHIP (UNLOCK YOUR GREATNESS PROGRAM)

SUGGESTED GRADES: Grades 8 - 12

UNIT: DEFINE..... THE LEADER IN YOU

LESSON 3

AIM: To introduce the main Principles of Leadership

LEARNING OBJECTIVES

At the end of the lesson, students will be able to:

1. Define the term "Influence"
2. State examples of Positive and Negative Influence
3. Explain the three Elements of Influence
4. Differentiate between Thoughts and Ideas
5. Describe thoughts that transform into ideas that move into action using own life experiences

LESSON CONTENT

- Definition of Influence

- Examples of Positive Influence

- Examples of Negative Influence

- Elements of Influence – Actions, Thoughts, Feelings

- Differences between Thoughts and Ideas

- Transformation of Thoughts into Ideas into Action (using own life experiences)

INSTRUCTIONAL PROCEDURES

Focusing Event

- "Stand by your Quote"
    a) Place thoughtful Quotes in large print on walls
    b) Provide a variety of different aspects of Leadership
    c) Leave plenty of room between Quotes
    d) Give each student an index card
    e) Ask students to leave their chairs and walk around the room reading Quotes
    f) Teacher's Instruction: "Stand by your Quote"
    g) Allow 5 minutes for them to explain on the Index Card, why his/her chosen Quote is important to them

Teaching Procedures

- Students will site good and bad examples from the Internet, Newspapers, Movie Theatres, Church, Community, Schools and Families
- During the lesson, students will be reminded of the importance of taking responsibility for their choices

Formative Check

- Students will share their Leadership Insights from their "Stand by your Quote" Activity with the class

Student Participation

- "Stand by your Quote" Activity
- Share Leadership Insights from "Stand by your Quote" Activity with the class

EVALUATION PROCEDURES

Create a table with five Thoughts leading to Ideas (according to guidelines on Page 24 in Textbook

MATERIALS AND AIDS

- "Stand by your Quote" Stickers
- Index Cards
- Textbooks

CLOSURE

Students will be instructed to own their Quote by writing their names on the Sticker.

INSTRUCTOR/TEACHER:

COURSE TITLE: LEADERSHIP (UNLOCK YOUR GREATNESS PROGRAM)

SUGGESTED GRADES: Grades 8 - 12

UNIT: DEFINE..... THE LEADER IN YOU

LESSON 4

AIM: To introduce the main Principles of Leadership

LEARNING OBJECTIVES:

At the end of the lesson, students will be able to:

1. State the "Great Leadership" Formula
2. Apply Leadership to daily experiences and responsibilities

LESSON CONTENT

"Great Leadership" Formula

Review of the terms "Ideas", "Vision", "Planned Actions", and "Influence"

INSTRUCTIONAL PROCEDURES

Focusing Event:

- Make a list of things that can happen when you do not have a plan

Teaching Procedures:

- Ask students to read Case Study (Alice Jones)
- Apply the Great Leadership Formula to the Case Study Questions
- Guided Class Discussion will follow

Formative Check

- Great Leadership Formula Activity – Pages 28 & 29
- Allows students to practice using every variable at the same time by listing three Visions they are very excited about and completing the table

Student Participation

- Great Leadership Formula Activity
- Case Study – Alice Jones (Textbook – Pages 30 – 32)
- Guided Class Discussion
- Exit Cards

EVALUATION PROCEDURES

- On Exit Cards (to be distributed, completed, and returned to the teacher), students will complete the following sentence:

  "I once believed leaders……………………………….. but now I know leaders………………………………………………………………………..

MATERIALS AND AIDS

- 4 x 6 Exit Cards
- Exit Card Box
- Textbook
- Dictionaries
- Markers
- Formula Sheet

CLOSURE

Teacher instructs students to deposit their Exit Cards in the Exit Box provided.

CHAPTER 2

INSTRUCTOR/TEACHER:

COURSE TITLE: LEADERSHIP (UNLOCK YOUR GREATNESS PROGRAM)

SUGGESTED GRADES: Grades 8 - 12

UNIT: DETERMINE….. YOUR INNATE INTELLIGENCE

LESSON 5

AIM: To evaluate the types of innate Intelligence

LEARNING OBJECTIVES

At the end of the lesson, students will be able to:

1. State the nine types of Intelligence
2. Outline the Problem-solving, Fact-finding, and Creative Skills involved in Verbal, Logical, and Visual Intelligence
3. Outline the Mind, Body and Soul Skills involved in Musical and Kinesthetic Intelligence

LESSON CONTENT

Types of Intelligence

- Verbal/Linguistic
- Logical/Mathematical
- Musical/Rhythmic
- Spatial/Visual
- Kinesthetic/Physical
- Interpersonal/Social
- Intrapersonal/Intuitive
- Naturalist/Nature
- Philosophical/Humanitarian

Problem-solving/Fact-finding and Creative Skills = Verbal/Logical/Visual Intelligence

Mind, Body and Soul Skills = Musical/Kinesthetic Intelligence

INSTRUCTIONAL PROCEDURES

Focusing Event

- Ask students – Do you consider yourself a) Investigative b) Artistic c) Social d) Enterprising e) Conventional f) Realistic
- Pair and Share Activity - Students will be given 5 minutes to share

- Guided Class Discussion will follow

Teaching Procedures

- Display a Chart with a list of the Nine Intelligences
- Ask students to place themselves in groups of two, and outline the following:
  a) Problem-solving, Fact-finding, and Creativity Skills involved in Verbal,

    Logical and Visual Intelligence
  b) Mind, Body and Soul Skills involved in Musical and Kinesthetic Intelligence

Formative Check

Pair and Share – Students will be instructed to share ideas on Problem-solving, Fact-finding, and Creativity Skills involved in Verbal, Logical and Visual Intelligence

Student Participation

- Guided Discussion
- Pair and Share

EVALUATION PROCEDURES

- "Stop and Reflect" – Textbook (Pages 39 & 40 - Questions 1, 2, 3 and 5)

MATERIALS AND AIDS

- "The Nine Types of Intelligence" Chart
- Textbook
- White Board

CLOSURE

- Remind students of the importance of knowing their mix of Intelligences

INSTRUCTOR/TEACHER:

COURSE TITLE: LEADERSHIP (UNLOCK YOUR GREATNESS PROGRAM)

SUGGESTED GRADES: Grades 8 - 12

UNIT: DETERMINE..... YOUR INNATE INTELLIGENCE

LESSON 6

AIM: To evaluate the types of innate Intelligence

LEARNING OBJECTIVES

At the end of the lesson, students will be able to:

1. Outline the Motivation, Empathy and Feelings Skills involved in Interpersonal, Interpersonal, and Naturalist Intelligence
2. Outline the History, Politics, Policies, and Guidelines Skills involved in Philosophical Intelligence
3. Display careers involved in the nine Types of Intelligence in the form of Group Presentations

LESSON CONTENT

- Motivation, Empathy and Feelings = Interpersonal, Intrapersonal and Naturalist Intelligence
- History, Politics, Guidelines = Philosophical Intelligence

INSTRUCTIONAL PROCEDURES

Focusing Event

- Ask students: How can the study of Intelligence point you in the right career direction?

Teaching Procedures

- Ask students to place themselves in the same group as the previous lesson, and outline the following:
  a) Motivation, Empathy, and Feelings Skills involved in Interpersonal, Intrapersonal, and Naturalist Intelligence
  b) History, Politics, and Guidelines Skills involved in Philosophical Intelligence
- Group Project Guidelines: Students will be placed in Four Groups and will be assigned as follows:
  1. Verbal/Logical/Visual Intelligence
  2. Musical/Kinesthetic Intelligence
  3. Intrapersonal/Interpersonal/Naturalist Intelligence
  4. Philosophical Intelligence

Students will be instructed to use Construction Paper and include Careers, Personality Traits, Graphics, Photos, relating to their topic.

Formative Check

Ask students to account for the role they play in the Group Presentation by providing a written List of Group Members and their roles.

Student Participation

- Pair and Share
- Group Project

EVALUATION PROCEDURES

Rubric Sheet for Group Presentation

MATERIALS AND AIDS

- Construction Paper
- Markers
- Magazines/Internet/Textbook
- Photos
- Graphics
- Scissors

- Glue

CLOSURE

- Students reminded of the due date for the Group Presentation and to pay attention to the Rubric (which was discussed in class).

INSTRUCTOR/TEACHER:

COURSE TITLE: LEADERSHIP (UNLOCK YOUR GREATNESS PROGRAM)

SUGGESTED GRADES: Grades 8 - 12

UNIT: DETERMINE..... YOUR INNATE INTELLIGENCE

LESSON 7

AIM: To evaluate the types of innate Intelligence

LEARNING OBJECTIVES

At the end of the lesson, students will be able to:

1. Analyse the Case Study 'Ade Beckley'
2. Prepare for Oral Group Presentations

LESSON CONTENT

Written Analysis of the Case Study 'Ade Beckley'
Oral Presentation Rubric – Organization, Creativity,

INSTRUCTIONAL PROCEDURES

Focusing Event

Ask students the following questions:

- What role did you play in your team?
- Did the project require a lot of time?

Teaching Procedures

- Students will be instructed to do a written class assignment: "Discuss any two issues from the Case Study"
- Students will be allowed time to prepare for Group Project

Formative Check

- Written Analysis of Case Study

Student Participation:

- Written Assignment – Case Study
- Group Project

EVALUATION PROCEDURES

- Rubric for Group Project (Teacher will distribute to students)

MATERIALS AND AIDS

- Textbook
- White Board
- Construction Paper
- Markers
- Magazines/Internet/Textbook
- Photos
- Graphics
- Scissors
- Glue

CLOSURE

- Allow students to provide feedback for the Group Project (Constructive Criticisms are also allowed).

INSTRUCTOR/TEACHER:

COURSE TITLE: LEADERSHIP (UNLOCK YOUR GREATNESS PROGRAM)

SUGGESTED GRADES: Grades 8 - 12

UNIT: DETERMINE..... YOUR INNATE INTELLIGENCE

LESSON 8

AIM: To evaluate the types of innate Intelligence

LEARNING OBJECTIVES

At the end of the lesson, students will be able to:

1. Differentiate among the nine Types of Intelligence

LESSON CONTENT

- "Stop and Reflect" – pgs 38 – 41
- Group Presentations – Groups 1 - 4

INSTRUCTIONAL PROCEDURES

Focusing Event

- Is it possible to speak five languages and when it comes to a waiter, you are entirely blank?

Teaching Procedures

- Ask students to complete "Stop and Reflect" in Textbook
- Group Presentations

Formative Check

"Stop and Reflect" in Textbook – pgs 38 - 41

Student Participation:

- Group Presentations

-

EVALUATION PROCEDURES

Groups will be marked for their Presentation according to the Rubric (discussed with students)

MATERIALS AND AIDS

- Textbook
- Tape

CLOSURE

- Ask students to think which Type of Intelligence, they would want to develop

CHAPTER 3

INSTRUCTOR/TEACHER:

COURSE TITLE: LEADERSHIP (UNLOCK YOUR GREATNESS PROGRAM)

SUGGESTED GRADES: Grades 8 - 12

UNIT: DISCOVER.....YOUR SOLUTIONS FOR THE WORLD'S PROBLEMS

LESSON 9

AIM: To assess solutions for the world's problems

LEARNING OBJECTIVES

At the end of the lesson, students will be able to:

1. Define the term "Potential"
2. Identify their strongest talents and skills
3. Discover how their gifts and talents can serve a solution to the world
4. Develop Gifts, Motivation, Passions, Character, Skills, and Destiny to achieve full potential

LESSON CONTENT

- Definition of Potential
- Individual Talents and Skills
- Ways to use individual talents and skills to serve a solution to the world

INSTRUCTIONAL PROCEDURES

Focusing Event

- Complete the "Talents and Skills" Table

Teaching Procedures

- Students will be given a 'Talents and Skills' Table to record five of their own talents and skills and also five talents and skills of Enia Netlan.
- Through guided discussions, students will discuss how one of the identified personal talents/skills and one of the identified talents and skills of Enia Netlan, will or have served a solution to the world

Formative Check

Case Study – Enia Netlan

Student Participation

- Completing the Talents and Skills Tables:
  a) Personal
  b) Enia Netlan

EVALUATION PROCEDURES

Unit Test

MATERIALS AND AIDS

- "Talents and Skills" Table - Personal
- "Talents and Skills" Table - Enia Netlan

CLOSURE

- Ask students if they are willing to commit themselves to a lifetime of personal growth.

CHAPTER 4

INSTRUCTOR/TEACHER:

COURSE TITLE: LEADERSHIP (UNLOCK YOUR GREATNESS PROGRAM)

SUGGESTED GRADES: Grades 8 - 12

UNIT: DEDICATE YOURSELF..... TO PURSUE PURPOSE

LESSON 10

AIM: To develop a Career Vision for life

LEARNING OBJECTIVES

At the end of the lesson, students will be able to:

1. State their Career Vision
2. Identify five struggles that present themselves when finding their core purpose
3. State the two Elements of Focus

LESSON CONTENT

- Career Vision

- Personal Life's Struggles

- Focus = Concentration + Priorities

- Concentration

- Priorities

INSTRUCTIONAL PROCEDURES

Focusing Event

- Figure out what your priorities are, and then concentrate on developing them.
- Where do we begin?

Teaching Procedures

- Ask students to create a Mind Map of their Career
- Students will include
  a) steps to getting there
  b) continuation education to move up the ladder, and
  c) connections needed to make career circles
  d) new mindset

Formative Check

- Mind Map will be collected for marking (according to guidelines outlined)

Student Participation

- Mind Map
- "Stop and Reflect"

EVALUATION PROCEDURES

- "Stop and Reflect" – Textbook (Questions 1 -3, Page 63)

MATERIALS AND AIDS

- Textbook
- Construction Paper
- Markers

CLOSURE

- Encourage students to pursue their unique purpose

INSTRUCTOR/TEACHER:

COURSE TITLE: LEADERSHIP (UNLOCK YOUR GREATNESS PROGRAM)

SUGGESTED GRADES: Grades 8 - 12

UNIT: DEDICATE YOURSELF..... TO PURSUE PURPOSE

LESSON 11

AIM: To develop a Career Vision for life

LEARNING OBJECTIVES

At the end of the lesson, students will be able to:

1. Discover true passion, natural abilities, and talents
2. Differentiate among the nine Public Leadership Roles in society

LESSON CONTENT

- Passion
- Natural Abilities
- Talents

- Types of Public Leadership Roles in society – Political, Social, Spiritual, Organizational, Business, Educational, Entertainment, Military, and Sports

INSTRUCTIONAL PROCEDURES

Focusing Event

- Ask students to walk around the room and on the "Talents and Abilities" Sheet provided, write down the name of a student who has the following talents and skills:
  a) Award Winner
  b) Plays a musical instrument
  c) Bilingual
  d) Left-handed
  e) Gymnastic abilities
  f) Swimming abilities
  g) Travelled to more than three countries
  h) From a Military background

Teaching Procedures

- Students will be introduced to the Public Leadership Roles in Society
- Students will be given instructions to complete the Matching Exercise on Public Leadership Roles in Society

- Guided Class Discussion

a) Case Study

b) Summary – Share things that they like, but are not good at

Formative Check

- Matching Exercise – Public Leadership Roles in Society
- Case Study: David Oyedepo - Group Discussion

Student Participation

- Matching Exercise
- Case Study
- "Stop and Reflect"

EVALUATION PROCEDURES

- "Stop and Reflect" (Textbook – Questions 4, 5 & 6 – Pages 63 & 64)

MATERIALS AND AIDS

- Textbook
- Matching Exercise on Public Leadership Roles
- "Talents and Abilities" Sheet

CLOSURE

- Ask students to share things they like, but are not good at.

CHAPTER 5

INSTRUCTOR/TEACHER:

COURSE TITLE: LEADERSHIP (UNLOCK YOUR GREATNESS PROGRAM)

SUGGESTED GRADES: Grades 8 -12

UNIT: DARE..... TO DEFINE YOUR OWN SUCCESS

LESSON 12

AIM: To assess personal success

LEARNING OBJECTIVES

At the end of the lesson, students will be able to:

1. State "Personal Success Statement"
2. List three Elements of Success
3. Compile a 5-page Autobiography of themselves

LESSON CONTENT

- Success Statement Guidelines
- Elements of Success – Passion, Natural Abilities, Talents
- 5-Page Autobiography Rubric

INSTRUCTIONAL PROCEDURES:

Focusing Event:

"True Success is individual, unique, and personal"

- Teacher will pass around a roll of Toilet Paper to the group and tell them to take as much as they need. No further explanation. Each person, when done, must tell a fact or something about themselves, for each square of Toilet Paper they took.

Teaching Procedures:

- Ask students to create a "My Personal Statement" on Construction Paper provided, which should include the following information:

  a) Achievements I am Proud of (Hobbies, Interests/Passion, Skills/Talents, Natural Abilities)
  b) Attributes that makes me Special/Unique/Interesting
  c) What I want from the Future

- Students will be given a Rubric and reminded of the following key points:

    a) Presentation Style
    b) Make it interesting
    c) Check Spelling and Grammar

- Students will be reminded that they must do their own work

- "My Personal Statement" will be collected at the end of the class

- Students will be given instructions for compiling the 5-Page Autobiography (including "My Personal Statement") and should take the following related materials to the next class:

    a) Pictures
    b) Family Tree
    c) Awards
    d) Certificates

Formative Check

- "My Personal Statement"

Student Participation

- Toilet Paper Activity
- "My Personal Statement"

EVALUATION PROCEDURES

- 5-Page Autobiography ("My Personal Statement" +) to be submitted in next class

MATERIALS AND AIDS

- Roll of Toilet Paper
- Construction Paper
- Markers
- Rubric for Autobiography

CLOSURE

- Ask students to interpret the proverb "A Mango cannot eat itself" Textbook – pg 72)

INSTRUCTOR/TEACHER:

COURSE TITLE: LEADERSHIP (UNLOCK YOUR GREATNESS PROGRAM)

SUGGESTED GRADES: Grades 8 - 12

UNIT: DARE..... TO DEFINE YOUR OWN SUCCESS

LESSON 13

AIM: To assess personal success

LEARNING OBJECTIVES

At the end of the lesson, students will be able to:

1. Compile 5-Page Autobiography

LESSON CONTENT

- Rubric for Autobiography

INSTRUCTIONAL PROCEDURES

Focusing Event

- Student will be asked the following question: In what ways do you think Parents and Teachers are helping you to succeed?

Teaching Procedures

- Students will be allowed the first 15 minutes of the class time to complete their Autobiography

- Pair and Share – Students will be placed in groups of two and will share their Autobiography with each other.

- Each student will share with the class, two things they learnt about their partner

Formative Check

- Group Sharing of 2 things they learnt about their partner

Student Participation

- Pair and Share
- Share with Group

EVALUATION PROCEDURES

- Autobiography will be collected and marked according to Rubric

MATERIALS AND AIDS

- Rubric for Autobiography

- Construction Paper

- Markers

- Tape

- Glue

- Scissors

CLOSURE

- Encourage students to gather samples (projects, autobiography) to validate the skills they are building

CHAPTER 6

INSTRUCTOR/TEACHER:

COURSE TITLE: LEADERSHIP (UNLOCK YOUR GREATNESS PROGRAM)

SUGGESTED GRADES: Grades 8 - 12

UNIT: DEVELOP..... YOUR CHARACTER

LESSON 14

AIM: To discover the achievements of great men and women in the world

LEARNING OBJECTIVES

At the end of the lesson, students will be able to:

1. Differentiate between Leaders and Significant World Leaders
2. State one achievement made by five great men and women in history

LESSON CONTENT

- Leaders v Significant World Leaders
- Achievement made by great men and women in history

INSTRUCTIONAL PROCEDURES

Focusing Event

- Leaders are those who had an opportunity to play central roles in the drama of their times, while significant World Leaders are those who played a successful role under times of great stress and change.
- Students will be instructed to complete the "World Leaders Word Scramble Sheet" – Unscramble the following names of great leaders

a) GINK _____   HARO   _____

b) DAXENLARE _____   HIDGAN _____

c) LAMDENA _____ ECRASA   _____

Teaching Procedures

- Students will be placed in five groups and each group given a sheet of paper of one of the following questions for them to brainstorm the answer as a group. One student will be selected from each group to walk around asking the other groups to provide the answer to their question until all questions are answered by each group.
- See Questions below:

1. King
   a) The first Queen of England known for trusting advisors to make good decisions
   b) The Roman General widely credited with the origin and leadership to transform Rome's Republic into an Empire
   c) Successfully promoted acts of non-violent disobedience that helped create equality in the form of human rights in US

2. Ghandi
   a) Maintained the US and helped to bring an end to slavery
   b) An Indian Nationalist who inspired the world with the use of non-violent protest to create change
   c) Voted a military genius and uniter of people of Southern Office

3. Reagan
   a) President of the US who focused on lowering taxes to produce economic growth
   b) Served 27 years in prison before becoming President of the same nation
   c) British Prime Minister whose leadership through Second World War is of great significance

4. Caesar
   a) Leader of the Chinese Revolution thought to be the key person establishing China as a world power

    b) The Roman General widely credited with the origin and leadership to transform Rome's Republic into an Empire

    c) Leader of the Shoguns in what is now considered Tokyo

5. Mandela

    a) An Indian Nationalist that inspired the world with the use of non-violent protest to create change

    b) Leader of the Aztec Empire

    c) Served 27 years in prison and rose to become South Africa 's first democratically-elected black President in post-apartheid

Formative Check

- Cooperative Group Learning

Student Participation:

- Cooperative Group Learning

EVALUATION PROCEDURES

- "Stop and Reflect" – Textbook (Pgs 83 – 85)

MATERIALS AND AIDS

- Textbook

- Five Question Sheets

- World Leaders Word Scramble Sheet

CLOSURE

- Discuss the statement "Whatever lives in your mind today will live in your future tomorrow."

CHAPTER 7

INSTRUCTOR/TEACHER:

COURSE TITLE: LEADERSHIP (UNLOCK YOUR GREATNESS PROGRAM)

SUGGESTED GRADES: Grades 8 - 12

UNIT: DEFEAT..... FEARS AND CHALLENGES

LESSON 15

AIM: To overcome fear

LEARNING OBJECTIVES

At the end of the lesson, students will be able to:

1. List five fears in relation to their Destiny
2. Discuss three ways in which fears can be overcome
3. Explain the two steps involved when facing challenges

LESSON CONTENT

- Fears in relation to Destiny

- Ways to overcome Fear
- Steps involved when facing Challenges

    a) Seek worthy counsel
    b) Develop the spirit of a marathon runner

INSTRUCTIONAL PROCEDURES

Focusing Event

- Starting in today's class, we will give upon all those things that no longer serve us, and we will embrace change. Are you ready?

Teaching Procedures

- Ask students to write down something they are afraid of – a fear they would want to overcome, for example, swimming, speaking in front of people
- Make a list of three small steps they think they can make to begin facing up to their fear

Formative Check

- "Stop and Reflect" – Textbook: pg 93 & 94

Student Participation

- "Stop and Reflect"
- Case Study – Mark Morrison

EVALUATION PROCEDURES

Case Study: Mark Morrison
- Discuss two challenges encountered by Mark and one way in which he overcame the challenge

MATERIALS AND AIDS

- Textbook

CLOSURE

- Thought: Do not blame others for your challenges, just fight

CHAPTER 8

INSTRUCTOR/TEACHER:

COURSE TITLE: LEADERSHIP (UNLOCK YOUR GREATNESS PROGRAM)

SUGGESTED GRADES: Grades 8 - 12

UNIT: DIALOGUE..... TO UNDERSTAND AND TO BE UNDERSTOOD

LESSON 16

AIM: To communicate the importance of verbal and written skills

LEARNING OBJECTIVES

At the end of the lesson, students will be able to:

1. Define Communication as an art and science
2. State the importance of verbal and written communication skills to great leaders
3. Compose Bio Poem

LESSON CONTENT

- Definition of Communication as a Science and Art
- Importance of Verbal and Written Communication Skills to great leaders

    a) Gather Personal Information – Bio Poem
    b) "Stand and Deliver" - Personal Elevator Speech

INSTRUCTIONAL PROCEDURES

Focusing Event

Did you know?

Words are 7% effective

Tone of voice is 38% effective

Non-verbal clues are 55% effective

Teaching Procedures

- Allow students 10 minutes to compose a Bio Poem in the suggested format below:

Your first name

Who is...........................2 words describing your strength

Who loves....................2 things you love to do

Who skills include.........2 things you are able to do

Who values.................2 things that are important to you

Who would like to have a job as ....or as...........2 jobs you would like

Resident.......................City where you live

Your last name

- Students will complete Case Study

Formative Check

- Bio Poem - Oral Presentation

Student Participation

- Bio Poem
- Case Study Written Analysis

EVALUATION PROCEDURES

- Case Study Analysis: Dr. Armand Thomas (Textbook: Pgs 102 & 103)

MATERIALS AND AIDS

- Textbook

CLOSURE

- Students will be encouraged to practise your 30 second "Elevator Speech".

INSTRUCTOR/TEACHER:

COURSE TITLE: LEADERSHIP (UNLOCK YOUR GREATNESS PROGRAM)

SUGGESTED GRADES: Grades 8 - 12

UNIT: DIALOGUE..... TO UNDERSTAND AND TO BE UNDERSTOOD

LESSON 17

AIM: To communicate the importance of verbal and written skills

LEARNING OBJECTIVES

At the end of the lesson, students will be able to:

1. Discuss six methods of delivering the message
2. Identify four Barriers to Communication
3. Outline the 12 Types of Non-Verbal Vocabulary

LESSON CONTENT

- Delivery of the Message
  a) Face-to-face meetings

b) Emails

c) Telephones/Voicemail

d) Video Conferences

e) Handwritten Letters

- Barriers to Communication

- Types of Non-Verbal Vocabulary

    a) Kinesics

    b) Proxemics

    c) Haptics

    d) Oculesics

    e) Chronemics

    f) Olfactics

    g) Vocalics

    h) Sound Symbols

    i) Silence

    j) Posture

    k) Adornment

    l) Locomotion

INSTRUCTIONAL PROCEDURES

Focusing Event:

- Do you communicate with your head or heart?

Teaching Procedures

- Tell students to look at the Communication Loop Chart

   a) Sender

   b) Message

   c) Receiver

   d) Feedback

- **QUESTION:** Name some of the ways we communicate

- **Suggested Answers:** Talking, Writing, Pictures

- Guided Class Discussion on "Delivering the Message"

- **QUESTION:** Have you been talking to someone and they misunderstood what you are saying? Why do you think that happened?

- External Barriers – noise, distractions, email not working, bad phone connection, time of day, use of too much technical words

- Internal Barriers – lack of interest in message, mistrust, fear, negative attitude, past experience, problems at home

Formative Check

- "Stop and Reflect" (Textbook, Pages 100 & 101)

Student Participation

- Guided Class Discussion
- Homework

EVALUATION PROCEDURES

- Homework: Explain three of the Non-Verbal Vocabulary, providing personal examples of each. (Due in the next class)

MATERIALS AND AIDS

- Communication Loop Chart
- Textbook

CLOSURE

- Each time you communicate, observe what you do, how it went, what went well, and how it could have improved.

CHAPTER 9

INSTRUCTOR/TEACHER:

COURSE TITLE: LEADERSHIP (UNLOCK YOUR GREATNESS PROGRAM)

SUGGESTED GRADES: Grades 8 - 12

UNIT: DELEGATE TEAMWORK..... TO MAKE THE DREAM WORK

LESSON 18

AIM: To evaluate the importance of Teamwork

LEARNING OBJECTIVES

At the end of the lesson, students will be able to:

1. List the Do's and Don'ts of Teamwork
2. Outline the four reasons for people not wanting to delegate
3. Explain the six requirements to fulfil a great vision

LESSON CONTENT

- Teamwork - Do's and Don'ts

    DO's

    1. Character

    2. Competence

    3. Passion

- **DON'Ts**

    1. Emotion

    2. Friendship

    3. Family

- **Reasons for people not wanting to Delegate**

    1. Ego

    2. Insecurity

    3. Ignorance

    4. Personality

- **Requirements for Teams to fulfil a great dream**

    1. Leadership

    2. Strategy

    3. Logistics

    4. Tactics

5. People

6. Structure

INSTRUCTIONAL PROCEDURES

Focusing Event

- From personal experience, would you prefer to fulfil your dreams by yourself or with others?

Teaching Procedures

- Ask students to complete the "Teamwork: Do's and Don'ts Activity.
- Instructions: Students will write two words that come to mind, beside each word in the Table
- Guided Class Discussion
- Students will be instructed to create a Poster with the Advantages and Disadvantages of Delegation to be submitted at the end of the class
- Read Case Study and identify the six Requirements that were needed to fulfill the dream

Formative Check

- Case Study: "My Story"

Student Participation

"Teamwork: Do's and Don'ts"

EVALUATION PROCEDURES

- Poster on Delegation

MATERIALS AND AIDS

- TEAMWORK: Do's and Don'ts Activity Sheet
- Construction Paper
- Markers
- Textbook

CLOSURE

- "Thought for the Day" - Progress and improvement comes with teamwork.

CHAPTER 10

INSTRUCTOR/TEACHER:

COURSE TITLE: LEADERSHIP (UNLOCK YOUR GREATNESS PROGRAM)

SUGGESTED GRADES: Grades 8 - 12

UNIT: DESIGN..... YOUR PLAN TO SUCCEED

LESSON 19

AIM: To Design a Vision of the Future

LEARNING OBJECTIVES

At the end of the lesson, students will be able to:

1. Identify the Principles of Strategic Thinking as the main ingredient of successful organizations

LESSON CONTENT

- Principles of Strategic Thinking
  1. Clarifying the direction and vision of the whole

2. Identifying relationships supporting the vision

3. Highlighting what is required for success

INSTRUCTIONAL PROCEDURES

Focusing Event

- What skills are learnt when playing a sport?

- Suggested answers: Motor skills, Math skills

- Ask students how Strategic Thinking is learnt

- To figure out plays

- The best way to get around a player

- Scoring a goal

Teaching Procedures

- "Stand by your Quote" is the big picture

- Place thoughtful quotes in large print on walls – leave plenty of room between Quotes

- Provide a wide variety of different aspects of Leadership

- Give each student an Index Card

- Ask students to leave their chairs and walk around the room reading the Quotes

- Have them stand by the Quote (more than one person can stand by a Quote)

- Allow 5 minutes for students to write the Quote and explain on the Index Card, why the chosen Quote is important to them

Formative Check

- Students will share their Leadership Insight according to the Principles of Strategic Thinking

Student Participation

EVALUATION PROCEDURES

- "Stop and Reflect" – Textbook (page 116)

MATERIALS AND AIDS

- Index Cards
- Quotes placed on walls

CLOSURE

- Encourage student to continue to actively plan and achieve some short term gains, which people will be able to see and celebrate

INSTRUCTOR/TEACHER:

COURSE TITLE: LEADERSHIP (UNLOCK YOUR GREATNESS PROGRAM)

SUGGESTED GRADES: Grades 8 - 12

UNIT: DESIGN..........YOUR PLAN TO SUCCEED

LESSON 20

AIM: To design a Vision of the Future

LEARNING OBJECTIVES

At the end of the lesson, students will be able to:

1. Outline the Steps to Success in the Strategic Thinking Model
2. Explain the Strategic Plan
3. Create a Portfolio with the best three

LESSON CONTENT

- Strategic Thinking: Steps to Success
  1. Vision the future
  2. Critical Processes

3. Purpose

4. Roles to be filled

5. Sequential Process

- Sample Strategic Plan
- Create Portfolio

INSTRUCTIONAL PROCEDURES

Focusing Event

- Thought for the Day: "Let the soul shine forth, demonstrating your magic."
- Students will review what they want to include in their Portfolios and select the best three pieces of work done during the year.

Teaching Procedures

- Students will be instructed to describe how each of the three pieces of work they select, "visions the future."
- Students will be instructed to refer to Strategic Plan (Textbook – Pages 116 – 118) and create a Portfolio.

Formative Check

- Selection of the three best pieces of work

Student Participation:

- Create a Portfolio entitled "Vision the Future"
- Guided Class Discussion

EVALUATION PROCEDURES

- Portfolio

MATERIALS AND AIDS

- Textbook
- Construction Paper
- Rubric for Portfolio

CLOSURE

- Personal Notes delivered to students at the end of the course.
- Thanks for letting the magic that is within you, shine through your Portfolios. You have shown what you know about life, writing, and the connections to that growing person which is "Unlocking the Greatness in You".

SPECIAL TIPS TO TEACHERS

For the "Unlock your Greatness" Program to be successfully taught, we have to begin by leading ourselves. As teachers, we want to help participants become great leaders of tomorrow, and you cannot just tell them to do it, you have to show it. This Manual is your Guide.

1. Draw on the best within us first, before assessing others.

> "Everyone thinks of changing the world but no one
> thinks of changing himself". Leo Tolstoy

2. Identify talents in people around you and work with them to create outstanding results for the team.

Participants will be motivated and eager to "unlock their greatness", but the following challenges can present themselves during the learning process:

a) Participants expect instant results

b) Group members can be uncooperative and start complaining about different things

Teachers can resolve these challenges by firstly, reminding participants that change does not happen instantly, but rather success is a gradual process and does not happen overnight, for example, exercising. Secondly, redirect the negative into positive. As the teacher, always keep classes moving forward in a positive direction. Thirdly, emphasize the importance of student participation and being prepared for classes. Be sure to explain this requirement at the start of the first lesson with reminders, if necessary.

As teachers, we must optimize our resources and maximize the potential of our participants, but it all starts with us leading the way to success. In closing, please be the best Leader you can be.

Igniting World Changers - Youth

Vision

To see young, passionate leaders successfully serving solutions to their communities.

Our Mission

To ignite leadership and greatness in young people.

Our Philosophy

1. The problems of a generation will never be greater than the ideas and solutions of the people born into that generation.

2. These ideas and solutions are within people in the form of an uncommon vision.

3. Many people do not know how to mine the gold (ideas and solutions within them), and add their greatest value to their communities.

4. It takes wisdom to mine the gold in you and fulfil an uncommon vision.

It is our passion to empower young people with wisdom to mine their gold and fulfil an uncommon vision.

Our Programs

1. Unlock your Greatness Program

This is a program for high schools and youth facilities where a leadership and visionary development curriculum is taught.

2. Ignite Vision Seminars

These are seminars designed to equip young men and women with the skills to develop a vision and a plan that unlocks the greatness in them.

3. Unlock your Greatness Rites of Passage Camps

The focus of these gender specific camps is to mentor, affirm and release teenage boys and girls into responsible manhood and womanhood.

Other Books by Greatness Publishing

Unlocking the Greatness Within

(A Young Leaders Handbook)

Uncommon Men and Distinguished Women

(A Rites of Passage Handbook for Young Men and Women)

The Gift of Political Leadership

The Gift of Organizational Leadership

The 12 Spheres of Leadership

(12 Types of Leaders That Shape The Destiny of Nations)

Discovering Me

www.ingramcontent.com/pod-product-compliance
Lightning Source LLC
Chambersburg PA
CBHW081156090426
42736CB00017B/3342